Looking at Literature Through Primary Sources™

The Adventures of Huckleberry Finn and Race in America

Jesse Jarnow

Published in 2004 by The Rosen Publishing Group, Inc.
29 East 21st Street, New York, NY 10010

First Edition

Unless otherwise attributed, all quotes in this book are excerpted from *The Adventures of Huckleberry Finn.*

Library of Congress Cataloging-in-Publication Data

Jarnow, Jesse.
The Adventures of Huckleberry Finn and race in America/Jesse Jarnow.
p. cm.—(Looking at literature through primary sources)
Summary: Traces the process and influences behind the writing of Mark Twain's novel *The Adventures of Huckleberry Finn*, which was published in the late nineteenth century and has been banned frequently since then for his use of racial epithets or simply for being coarse.
Includes bibliographical references and index.
ISBN 0-8239-4503-0 (lib. bdg.)
1. Twain, Mark, 1835–1910. *Adventures of Huckleberry Finn.* 2. United States—Race relations—History—19th century. 3. Twain, Mark, 1835–1910—Political and social views. 4. Satire, American—History and criticism. 5. Finn, Huckleberry (Fictitious character). 6. Race relations in literature. 7. Race in literature. [1. Twain, Mark, 1835–1910. *Adventures of Huckleberry Finn.* 2. Satire—History and criticism. 3. United States—Race relations—History—19th century. 4. Race in literature.]
I. Title. II. Series.
PS1305.J37 2003
813'.4—dc22
2003015890

Manufactured in the United States of America

On the cover: at top, a portrait of Samuel Clemens (Mark Twain), circa 1900; at bottom left, a photograph of a family of slaves picking cotton in a field near Savannah, Georgia, around 1860; and at bottom right, the cover of the original edition of *The Adventures of Huckleberry Finn.*

CONTENTS

INTRODUCTION

"We are suspicious of the middle-aged person who has not read *Huckleberry Finn*," wrote a Philadelphia newspaper editor in the late nineteenth century. "We envy the young person who still has it in store."

Called the great American novel by some, *The Adventures of Huckleberry Finn* captures the breadth of American life within its pages. More than 100 years since it was written, *Huckleberry Finn* continues to be relevant and enthralling. Published in the United States in 1885, *The Adventures of Huckleberry Finn* was written by Mark Twain, a pen name for humorist Samuel Langhorne Clemens. On the surface, it appears to be a children's story. Previous to *Huckleberry Finn*, Twain published the wildly successful *Adventures of Tom Sawyer*, a volume intended for younger readers. At first, *Huckleberry Finn* appeared to be a sequel. Huck, a delightful and good-hearted scamp, sets out on a raft journey down the mighty Mississippi River. Accompanied by a runaway slave named Jim, he undergoes a series of humorous adventures.

But *The Adventures of Huckleberry Finn* is not a book just for young readers. Mark Twain was a popular satirist known for scathing portraits of society. He toured widely as a lecturer, drawing huge audiences wherever he went. The novel is filled with far-reaching social criticism that penetrates nearly every facet of life in the American South in the years leading up to the Civil War. *Huckleberry Finn* is a book as much for adults as it is for children.

The author grew up on the banks of the Mississippi and spent many years working along the river. As an observer of the thriving culture that evolved around the river, Twain was second to none. In *Huckleberry Finn*, he animates the teeming and often lurid life with startling liveliness. His vivid characters engage in subtle debates and act out exaggerated morality tales. The result is a rare blend of page-turning excitement and exacting intellectual stimulation.

At the core of the book are Huck and Jim. It is their relationship and their travels on the river that drive the story. Both of them exist as outsiders to civilized society. Huck is the happy homeless son of the town drunk, constantly running away from all attempts to "sivilize" him. Jim is a slave escaping to freedom in the North. Their positions on the margins allow them unique perspectives on southern life.

The Adventures of Huckleberry Finn

Chapter I.

YOU don't know about me, without you have read a book by the name of "The Adventures of Tom Sawyer," but that ain't no matter. That book was made by Mr. Mark Twain, and he told the truth, mainly. There was things which he stretched, but mainly he told the truth. That is nothing. I never seen anybody but lied, one time or another, without it was Aunt Polly, or the widow, or maybe Mary. Aunt Polly—Tom's Aunt Polly, she is—and Mary, and the Widow Douglas, is all told about in that book—which is mostly a true book; with some stretchers, as I said before.

THE WIDOW'S.

Now the way that the book winds up, is this: Tom and me found the money that the robbers hid in the cave, and it made us rich. We got six thousand dollars apiece—all gold. It was an awful sight of money when it was piled up. Well, Judge Thatcher, he took it and put it out at interest, and it fetched us a dollar a day apiece, all the year round—more than a body could tell what to do with. The Widow Douglas, she took me for her son, and allowed she would sivilize me; but it was rough living in the house all the time, considering how dismal regular and decent the widow was in all her ways; and so when I couldn't stand it no longer, I lit out. I got into my old rags, and my sugar-hogshead again, and was free and satisfied. But

2

◆◆◆ **At the beginning of *The Adventures of Huckleberry Finn,* the narrator, Huck, tells the reader that he appeared in Mark Twain's earlier work *The Adventures of Tom Sawyer,* which was published in 1876. This is the illustrated opening page from the first edition of *The Adventures of Huckleberry Finn.***

The book is not "about" any one topic. Mark Twain's vision was too broad for that. One important theme, one that remains current even when removed from the context of the 1800s, is that of race. As a black man—either as a slave or as a free man—Jim faces terrible racism and oppression. By creating Jim as a compassionate character, Twain added a subtle antiracist argument to the national dialogue.

For this reason and others, the book was considered highly controversial when it was published. As a testament to its power, some schools still ban the book! It is a greater mark that even more people are still reading it.

Chapter 1

The Life of Mark Twain

Mark Twain was born Samuel Langhorne Clemens on November 30, 1835, in Florida, Missouri. When he was four, his family moved 40 miles (64.4 kilometers) to the east, to Hannibal, a town on the western bank of the Mississippi River. Twain's childhood in Hannibal would eventually provide the basis for many of his popular writings. In *The Adventures of Tom Sawyer* and *The Adventures of Huckleberry Finn*, Hannibal would be transformed into St. Petersburg.

In *Huck Finn*, the author describes a wistful view of the town from above, as Huck and Tom Sawyer climb to an overlook.

> **Well, when Tom and me got to the edge of the hill-top, we looked away down into the village and could see three or four lights twinkling, where there was sick folks, may be; and the stars over us was sparkling ever so fine; and down by the village was the river, a whole mile broad, and awful still and grand.**

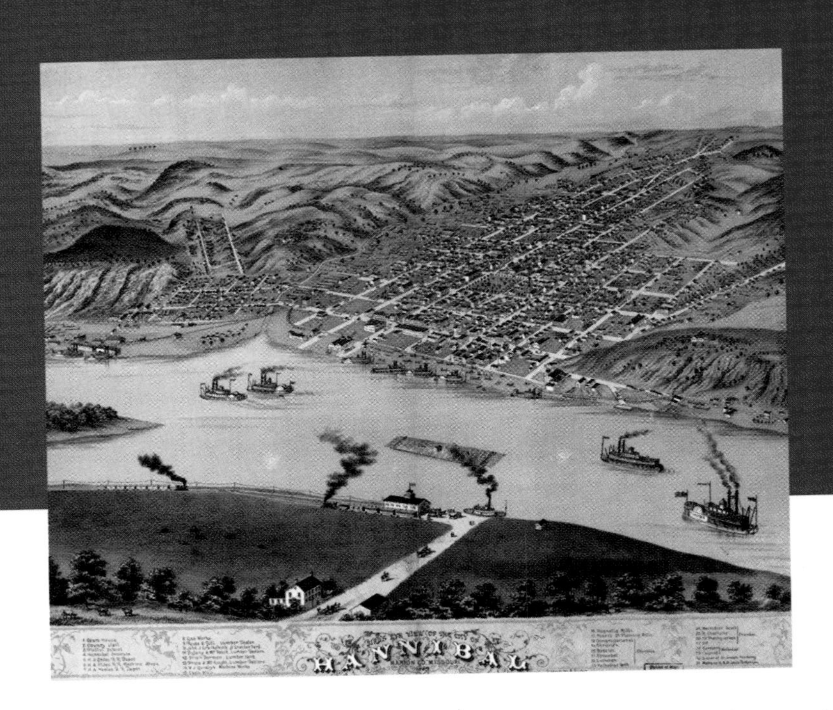

Albert Ruger created this lithograph of the town of Hannibal as he saw it in 1869, fourteen years after Samuel Clemens had left the town. As is depicted here, Hannibal was still a bustling town, primarily because of its location along the bank of the Mississippi River.

One can imagine a young Twain looking out over Hannibal. The town below was populated by dozens of residents who would later be turned into characters. A boy named Tom Blankenship provided the inspiration for Huck. (Twain took the last name "Finn" from Jimmy Finn, Hannibal's town drunk.)

As a child, Twain listened to tales told by Jenny, the Twains' slave. Later in life, Twain would fondly sing spirituals he remembered Jenny singing. Slavery was nearing its peak during

♦♦♦ This portrait of Samuel Clemens was taken when he was fifteen years old and a printer's apprentice. It is the earliest known portrait of the famous author.

Twain's childhood. Like Huck, Twain's opinions about the institution evolved over time.

When Twain was eleven, his father died. To support the family, he went to work as a printer's apprentice. It was there that he began to receive an important part of his education. As a printer, Twain was exposed to hundreds of books, political pamphlets, religious tracts, and handbills. This array of influences played a huge role in Twain's writing. As an adult, he wrote fluently on dozens of topics.

Falling in Love with the River

In 1855, when he was seventeen, Twain set off from Hannibal. With his skills as a printer, he traveled across the country, working in New York City; St. Louis, Missouri; and Cincinnati, Ohio.

After some time traveling, he decided that he would like to explore the Amazon in South America. To begin his journey, he boarded a steamboat to head south on the Mississippi. On that fateful trip, he fell in love with the river. By 1857, Twain was a licensed steamboat operator. They were idyllic days for Twain. His experiences influenced his writing in *Huckleberry Finn*, *Tom Sawyer*, *Life on the Mississippi*, and dozens of short articles. Twain always spoke romantically of life on the Mississippi.

He wrote the following in *Huckleberry Finn*.

> **Two or three days and nights went by; I reckon I might say they swum by, they slid along so quiet and smooth and lovely . . . It was a monstrous big river down there—sometimes a mile and a half wide . . . soon as night was most gone, we stopped navigating and tied up—nearly always in the dead water under a tow-head; and then cut young cottonwoods and willows and hid the raft with them. Then we set out the lines. Next we slid into the river and had a swim, so as to freshen up and cool off; then we set down on the sandy bottom where the water was about knee deep, and watched the daylight come. Not a sound, anywheres—perfectly still—just like the whole world was asleep, only sometimes the bull-frogs a-cluttering, maybe.**

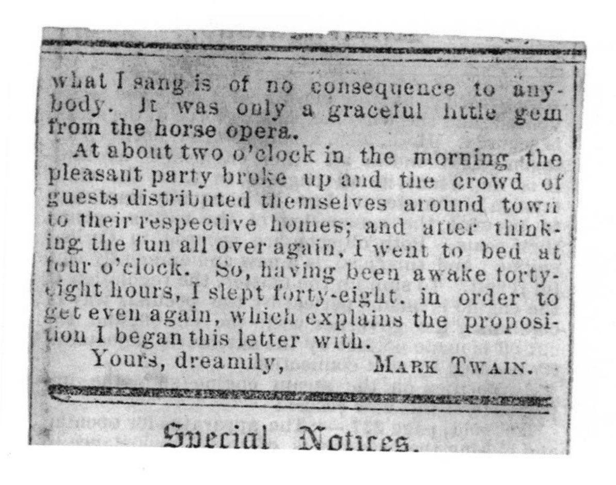
what I sang is of no consequence to anybody. It was only a graceful little gem from the horse opera.

At about two o'clock in the morning the pleasant party broke up and the crowd of guests distributed themselves around town to their respective homes; and after thinking the fun all over again, I went to bed at four o'clock. So, having been awake forty-eight hours, I slept forty-eight, in order to get even again, which explains the proposition I began this letter with.

Yours, dreamily, MARK TWAIN.

Special Notices.

♦♦♦ **The pen name Mark Twain first appeared in *Territorial Enterprise*, a Nevada newspaper for which Samuel Clemens wrote articles in the form of letters. Shown here is a portion of a page from the paper's February 3, 1863, edition.**

Adopting a Pen Name

In 1861, as the Civil War broke out, traffic on the river was interrupted. Twain, who was still known as Samuel Clemens, enlisted in the Confederate army, though he deserted it after a week. He fled to Nevada. After trying his hand at prospecting, he moved on to journalism. He traveled from place to place, writing for several papers.

While working in Carson City, Nevada, Clemens decided that he needed a pen name. He thought back to his days on the river. One of his jobs as a river man was to measure the water depth, to see if the steamboat could pass through. This was done by dropping a marked rope into the water. If the water was deep enough—two fathoms (12 feet, or 3.7 meters)—the boat operator would call out "by the mark twain!" and the boat would pass. In 1863, Clemens adopted Mark Twain as his pen name. Though his friends and acquaintances knew him as Sam Clemens, the public knew him as Mark Twain.

"ROUNDING A BEND" ON THE MISSISSIPPI.

1875.] *Old Times on the Mississippi.* 69

the utmost respectability, has been, throughout the period of Miss Florence Cook's mediumship, her constant friend and supporter. Many of her sittings were held at his town-house, 16 Gloucester Square, Hyde Park, London.

Now, in The (London) Spiritualist of February 1, 1873, Mr. Luxmore has given, under his own signature, the full details of a séance, by the Holmeses, which he attended on the evening of January 12, 1873. After describing a preliminary dark séance, and then the appearance, in the light at the aperture, of four or five faces, "very plainly seen," he adds: "Last of all came Katie, who generally, or I believe I may say always, presents herself at Miss Cook's séances. I have seen her three times at Hackney,[1] and could perfectly identify the face. She spoke, as usual, in a whisper, but not sufficiently loud for me to determine what was said. I, although I had not the *slightest doubt of her identity*, said: 'If you are Katie, put out your chin as you do at Miss Cook's.' This was at once done. I should think it perfectly impossible for any one who has had the privilege of attending Miss Cook's séances to have a single doubt of its being the same face we see there." The italics are Mr. Luxmore's.

But all those who, like myself, were fortunate enough to converse frequently and familiarly with Katie last summer, will bear me out in asserting that the one peculiarity which marked her appearance at the aperture was, that each time, after she had said something to us, she withdrew the upper part of her face and head, bringing her chin prominently forward. The self-same peculiarity marks her recent reappearance.

It does not at all affect the genuine character of the phenomena whether we conclude that the question of identity is determined, or that it must be left open. Nor do I assert that it is *positively* settled by the above facts. What I do say is, that these facts, taken in connection with other evidence already adduced, afford to my mind fair and reasonable assurance that (though varying in outward feature) the spirit which conversed with Mr. Crookes and others in London and that which has spoken to myself and others here — in both cases an eminent instrument to advance the cause of Spiritualism — is but one and the same.

Robert Dale Owen.

[1] Where Miss Cook and her parents then lived. Katie, at that time, had not appeared in full form.

OLD TIMES ON THE MISSISSIPPI.

I.

When I was a boy, there was but one permanent ambition among my comrades in our village on the west bank of the Mississippi River. That was, to be a steamboatman. We had transient ambitions of other sorts, but they were only transient. When a circus came and went, it left us all burning to become clowns; the first negro minstrel show that came to our section left us all suffering to try that kind of life; now and then we had a hope that if we lived and were good, God would permit us to be pirates. These ambitions faded out, each in its turn; but the ambition to be a steamboatman always remained.

Once a day a cheap, gaudy packet arrived upward from St. Louis, and another downward from Keokuk. Before these events had transpired, the day was glorious with expectancy; after they had transpired, the day was a dead and empty thing. Not only the boys, but the whole village, felt this. After all these years I can picture that old time to myself now, just as it was then: the white town drowsing in the sunshine of a summer's morning; the streets empty, or pretty nearly so; one or two clerks sitting in front of the Water Street

At right, a page from the *Atlantic Monthly* of January 1875 bears the first installment of Mark Twain's *Old Times on the Mississippi,* which describes life as a pilot of a steamboat (an example of which is shown on the left).

Publishing and Lecturing

By 1864, Twain was living in San Francisco, California, and publishing regularly. He wrote humorous stories and sketches. He also began his career as a lecturer. Throughout his life, he would tour the world, giving deadpan readings, as well as publishing stories chronicling his travels. He moved east and settled in Hartford, Connecticut. Throughout the 1870s, he published a series of nonfiction books. In 1876, he put out his first novel, *The Adventures of Tom Sawyer*. Created for children, the book was a sentimental look at Twain's childhood in Hannibal.

Looking for Inspiration

Twain traveled up and down the Mississippi several times looking for inspiration. In addition to *Tom Sawyer*, these trips manifested themselves in a series of articles he published in the *Atlantic Monthly*. They were also becoming the primary research for what would become *The Adventures of Huckleberry Finn*. The nonfiction *Atlantic Monthly* articles—which were later published as *Life on the Mississippi*—and Twain's early work on *Huckleberry Finn* became entangled. Some chapters from *Huckleberry Finn* began as part of *Life on the Mississippi* and vice versa.

The stories were composed of sketches, detailing characters and scenes. Many of the smaller chunks of *Huckleberry Finn* could be read as travel journalism.

> **Every night we passed towns, some of them away up on black hillsides, nothing but just a shiny bed of lights, not a house could you see. The fifth night we passed St. Louis, and it was like the whole world lit up. In St. Petersburg, they used to say there was twenty or thirty thousand people in St. Louis, but I never believed it till I see that wonderful spread of lights at two o'clock that still night. There warn't a sound there; everybody was asleep.**

"It almost made the water in our ice-pitcher muddy as I read it," Twain's editor and friend William Dean Howells wrote in

Banned in the Twentieth Century

Throughout the twentieth century, *The Adventures of Huckleberry Finn* was frequently banned for Twain's repeated use of the word "nigger." The racial epithet was already considered offensive by the time of the book's publication in the late 1800s and only became more so as the years passed. Many have claimed that Twain's choice of the word undermines any antiracist argument he may have tried to make. The issue at hand, however, is context. Any other choice of words for a story set on the Mississippi River in the 1830s would be false.

It is an irony that Twain's book was accused of that which it was trying to prevent. "It [the accusation] struck me as a purist yet elementary kind of censorship designed to appease adults rather than educate children," wrote author Toni Morrison. "A serious comprehensive discussion of the term by an intelligent teacher certainly would have benefited my eighth-grade class and would have spared all of us (a few blacks, many whites—mostly second-generation immigrant children) some grief. Name calling is a plague of childhood and a learned activity ripe for discussion as soon as it surfaces."

praise. It was after this trip that Twain began work on *Huckleberry Finn*. It would be a difficult process.

Written in Three Sections

Twain wrote *The Adventures of Huckleberry Finn* in three separate sections, each with its own tone. The first part, written between 1875 and 1876, is a sweet boyhood reminiscence, ending after a riverboat destroys Huck and Jim's raft. The second part, conceived in 1879 and 1880, ends with an attempted lynching and thus moves into the realm of social commentary. The last section, composed between 1883 and 1885, is satire to the point of parody.

The Adventures of Huckleberry Finn Is Banned

In 1885, the Concord Free Library in Concord, Massachusetts, was the first to ban *The Adventures of Huckleberry Finn*. Calling the book "coarse" and "the veriest trash," the library committee removed it from the shelves.

Other libraries around the country banned the book, too. They believed that it was immoral. It wasn't that Huck was helping to free Jim from slavery. It was more that the pictures Twain sketched of the antebellum South were grotesque. Huck swore, stole fruit from farmers' pastures, swam naked in the Mississippi River, and lived a free lifestyle. This offended some people.

♦♦♦ This portrait of Mark Twain's family was taken in the early to middle 1880s. From left to right are Twain's daughter Clara; his wife, Livy; his daughter Jean; Twain himself; and his daughter Susy.

Fellow writers and editors came to Twain's defense. The *San Francisco Chronicle* commented, "There is a large class of people who are impervious to a joke, even when told by as consummate a master of the art of narration as Mark Twain." The author himself was deeply amused by all the ballyhoo. He called it a "generous action" and laughed that it would "sell 25,000 copies for us sure."

A Life of Misfortunes

During his life, Twain was plagued by a series of misfortunes—including the deaths of several of his children and the failure of his own publishing house and investments in a doomed printing press. By 1894, Twain found himself deeply in debt. Though his wife's health was failing, he was forced to tour the world giving lectures in order to work himself back to financial stability. Increasingly, his writing mirrored his mood. Twain died in 1910.

Chapter 2

Big River

Depending on whom you ask, the Mississippi River runs between 2,300 and 2,500 miles (3,701.5–4,023.4 km), from Lake Itasca in Minnesota to where it pours into the Gulf of Mexico in New Orleans, Louisiana. In the early nineteenth century, when Mark Twain was growing up in Hannibal, Missouri, the river was extremely important. Before the spread of railroads in the years after the Civil War, its currents provided the fastest mode of transportation for goods and people. Likewise, before enterprising men built a national telegraph network, information could travel only as fast as people. Thus, the Mississippi was also the quickest way to spread news and information.

Towns prospered along the river's banks. Between 1835 and 1845, when *The Adventures of Huckleberry Finn* is set, the population of Missouri nearly doubled, from around 250,000 to almost 500,000. An entire culture grew. It is this culture that Mark Twain captures in *Huckleberry Finn*. But, despite the common body of water and the way of life it created, life on the river

High Water Everywhere

There are many exaggerated elements in *The Adventures of Huckleberry Finn.* The scene where Huck and Jim encounter a house floating down the river is not one of them. Every year, the river undergoes what is called "the June rise." Snow melts in the mountains near the source of the river, and the excess water rolls off to the south. For residents of towns along the banks of the Mississippi, it was a way of life. Twain described it in *Life on the Mississippi:* "The whole vast face of the stream was black with drifting dead logs, broken boughs, and great trees that had caved in and been washed away."

For some, like Huck, the river could be bountiful. "The June rise used to be always luck for me," Huck says. "As soon as that rise begins, here comes cord-wood floating down, and pieces of log rafts—sometimes a dozen logs together; so all you have to do is catch them and sell them to the wood yards and the sawmill." Just as the river would ultimately provide Huck and Jim's escape route, it also provides their means of escape: their raft.

There were many different boats along the Mississippi. Some of them were simply designed, and some were more complex. Many were of European origin, though some were modeled after the boats of the American Indians. They ranged from small (like Huck and Jim's raft) up to almost 100 feet (30 m) in length (and capable of carrying fifty tons of cargo).

The floods could also be extremely dangerous. In 1851, when Twain was fifteen and working at the *Hannibal Western Union*, a local newspaper, it was particularly bad. "The great river is pitching, roaring, and tumbling through the streets, as if wholly unconscious of being an intruder!" the paper reported. "Altogether things look squally all about here—so much so, that if you don't get any paper next week, you may set it down that we are in the Mississippi! If there is a room to rent on the second or third story of any good business house on Main Street, we should be glad to be informed of the fact!"

was very different in the North than it was in the South. And in between—such as in Hannibal—it was even different from that.

Slavery in the Deep South

The temperate weather in the South allowed for year-round farming. This led planters to build huge plantations to harvest crops such as tobacco, which often required hundreds of men to operate. This is one of the reasons that slavery flourished in

This engraving depicts slaves harvesting sugar cane on a Louisiana plantation. In *Huckleberry Finn,* Jim runs away because he fears being sold "down the river." Conditions were especially harsh on the cane fields in states such as Louisiana in the Deep South.

the South. By the time of Twain's youth, slavery had become institutionalized in the South. As the North became industrialized, slavery became increasingly less necessary. This created a deep divide between the North and the South. This tension is what drives the plot of *Huckleberry Finn.*

In southern Missouri, where Twain, and Huck, lived, slavery still existed. However, there were few plantations. Mostly, slaves performed household duties, such as cooking and cleaning. They often worked alongside family members. The Deep South, with its sprawling fields, hot weather, and reputation for masters abusing slaves, seemed like hell on Earth.

Being sold down the river was a constant threat. Slave owners—such as Miss Watson, who owns Jim in *Huck Finn*—could hold it menacingly over their slaves' heads. This is precisely what causes Jim to run away.

> **Ole Missus—dat's Miss Watson—she pecks on me all de time, en treats me pooty rough, but she awluz said she wouln' sell me down to [New] Orleans. But I noticed dey wuz a nigger trader roun' de place considable, lately, en I begin to git oneasy. Well, one night, I creeps to de do', pooty late, en de do' warn't quite shet, en I hear ole missus tell de widder she gwnyne to sell me down to Orleans, but she didn' want to, but she could git eight hund'd dollars for me, en it 'uz sich a big stack o' money she couldn' resis'.**

♦♦♦ Miss Watson, the slave owner, is depicted holding a stern posture in this illustration by Edward Windsor Kemble, which appeared in the first edition of *The Adventures of Huckleberry Finn.*

Jim escapes. With Huck, he plans to drift down the river towards Cairo, Illinois, to board a steamboat for the North, where he will be free.

Speaking and Writing in Dialects

Like many of the characters in *Huckleberry Finn,* Jim speaks in nonstandard English. Twain was precise about how his characters spoke. *Huckleberry Finn* is set on a very specific chunk of the Mississippi River, from northern Missouri to southern Mississippi. As a native of the area, Twain researched speech patterns meticulously. He wanted his characters to speak accurately.

Existing manuscripts reveal literally thousands of small rewrites. Twain even added a humorous note to the front of the book, explaining his work.

In this book a number of dialects are used, to wit: the Missouri negro dialect; the extremest form of the backwoods South-Western dialect; the ordinary 'Pike-County' dialect; and four modified varieties of this last. The shadings have not been done in a hap-hazard fashion, or by guess-work; but pains-takingly, and with the trustworthy guidance and support of personal familiarity with these several forms of speech.

I make this explanation for the reason that without it many readers would suppose that all of these characters were trying to talk alike and not succeeding.

In nineteenth-century Missouri, one could travel from place to place and hear the English language sound as different as the environment looked. These regional variations are called dialects. Twain attempted to represent these dialects phonetically, by spelling out the various ways of pronouncing words. One can understand the dialects more easily by reading them aloud.

Twain focused particularly on the southern part of the river. "We was down south in the warm weather, now, and a mighty long ways from home," Huck says. "We begun to come to trees with Spanish moss on them, hanging down from the limbs like long grey beards. It was the first I ever see it growing, and it made the woods look solemn and dismal."

In his journal, Twain kept a list of topics he wished to focus on. One of the main ways that Twain hoped to provide antiracist

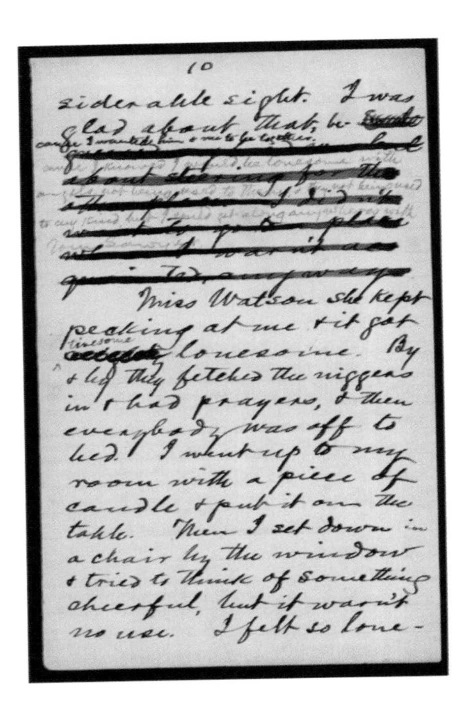
10
siderable sight. I was
glad about that, be-
Miss Watson she kept
pecking at me & it got
tiresome lonesome. By
& by they fetched the niggers
in & had prayers, & then
everybody was off to
bed. I went up to my
room with a piece of
candle & put it on the
table. Then I set down in
a chair by the window
& tried to think of something
cheerful, but it warn't
no use. I felt so lone-

This is a marked-up page from Mark Twain's original draft of *The Adventures of Huckleberry Finn.* Twain labored on and off for eight years before completing his manuscript and made thousands of revisions to develop his characters and to fine-tune the plot.

arguments was by revealing the hypocrisy of southern culture. (Northerners weren't exempt from Twain's satire, they simply weren't appropriate subject matter for *Huckleberry Finn.*)

The topic list was long and touched on many facets of southern life: the antidrinking temperance movement, violent family feuds, religion, folklore, and many others. This, especially, was Twain's goal in the middle sections of the book. In these places, the book becomes less about Huck and Jim and more about their environment. Huck is more of a narrator and less of a character.

Soon, two characters join Huck and Jim on their raft. The King and the Duke are confidence men—they skip from town to town, attempting to scam people out of their money. "They done a lecture on temperance," Huck says, revealing their two-facedness, "but they didn't make enough for them both to get drunk on."

It wasn't just the confidence men who were hypocritical, though. When Huck arrives at the Phelpses' farm, at the beginning of the book's last segment, he lies to his "Aunt" Sally about why he is late. He explains to her that the steamboat he was traveling on broke down.

> **"It warn't the grounding—that didn't keep us back but a little. We blowed out a cylinder-head."**
> **"Good gracious! Anybody hurt?"**
> **"No'm. Killed a nigger."**
> **"Well, it's lucky; because sometimes people do get hurt."**

Most white people did not think of slaves as humans. This was a fundamental view held in the South. If a slave died, it was not considered a loss of life. It was treated as a loss of property. Twain witnessed this indifference firsthand growing up. He often spoke of an incident in which he saw a slave get killed. "Nobody in the village approved of that murder, but of course no one said much about it," he later wrote.

Chapter 3

The Chain of Slaves

In 1840, the population of Missouri hovered near 380,000. Almost 60,000 of those people were slaves. Because of its geographic location, Missouri was an unusual slave state. Plantations could not survive in its climate, so there were only a few people who owned a lot of slaves. White slave owners usually owned only three or four slaves. And most people in Missouri didn't own slaves at all. In the Deep South, states often had fifty-two slaves for every hundred whites.

The slaves who lived in Missouri were required to perform many kinds of tasks. Farther south, the work was more repetitive. Missouri farmers grew a variety of crops, including hemp, wheat, corn, oats, and tobacco. Slaves tended to these crops in fields. Because of the long winters, slaves in Missouri were often trained to do other jobs. Many slaves served as carpenters, cooks, nurses, and maids. Though Missouri slaves were still treated extremely poorly, they were more integrated into the fabric of a town's life than were those farther South.

Slaves lived in a variety of housing. In a smaller family, a slave might have a room in the house. More frequently, though,

♦♦♦ In this illustration by Edward Windsor Kemble, Jim reacts in fear when he encounters Huck, whom he believes died several days earlier. Kemble, who drew all 174 illustrations for the first edition of *The Adventures of Huckleberry Finn,* was a young, struggling artist when he was commissioned for the project in 1884.

slaves would have their own quarters. Slave cabins were poorly constructed, often of logs, and were exceedingly hot in the summer and bitterly cold in the winter. Most of the time, the one-room buildings had the hard dirt of the ground instead of flooring. There was little comfort and little privacy.

Twain provides a description of the slave quarters on the Phelpses' farm, deep in Mississippi, which was relatively humane compared to how wretched some were known to have been.

> **[There was a] big double log house for the white folks . . . three little log nigger-cabins in a row t'other side the smoke-house; one little hut all by itself away down against the back fence, and some out-buildings down a piece the other side; ash-hopped, and big kettle to bile soap in, by the little hut; bench by the kitchen door, with bucket of water and a gourd; hound asleep there, in the sun; more hounds asleep, round about.**

Fables of the Reconstruction

Throughout *The Adventures of Huckleberry Finn,* Mark Twain often parodies several literary genres. One particular target of his is a style that arose in the mid-1870s. A spate of books romanticized the plantation system of the antebellum South, such as J. W. DeForest's *Kate Beaumont.* The popularity of this style continued well into the twentieth century, with the successful publication of Margaret Mitchell's 1936 novel, *Gone With the Wind.* The epic 1939 movie adaptation, starring Clark Gable and Vivien Leigh, presented an unrealistic vision of the Old South in startling Technicolor.

The film's introduction provides as good a summary of the view as any: "There was a land of cavaliers and cotton fields called the Old South. Here in this pretty world, gallantry took its last bow. Here was the last ever to be seen of knights and their ladies fair, of master and of slave." In the film, southern belle Scarlet O'Hara (Leigh) sees her home ravaged by war. In the end, she yearns for Tara, her family's estate. While the plantation may have been an idyllic place for her to grow up, it certainly wasn't for the family's slaves.

And though the film was supposed to be a vision of the Old South, the South of 1939 was not so far removed from what it had always been. Though the plantations and aristocracy were gone, the racism remained. When the film premiered in Atlanta, Georgia, in 1939, black actress Hattie McDaniel, who played the slave Mammy, could not attend. The theater was segregated.

In 2002, novelist Alice Randall published *The Wind Done Gone*. The novel is a retelling of *Gone With the Wind* from the perspective of the slaves at Tara. The novel speaks of intrigues and hidden stories occurring behind the scenes of *Gone With the Wind*. The book raised a great deal of controversy. The estate of Margaret Mitchell sued Randall's publishing company in an attempt to prevent its publication. The lawyers for Mitchell's estate argued that Randall had borrowed so much from *Gone With the Wind* that her book was in effect an unauthorized sequel. In response, Randall argued that her book was a parody.

An Atlanta district court held the book back from publication, but its decision was overturned on appeal.

The Life of a Slave

Throughout the week, slaves were worked from sunup to sundown. Usually, they were given Sundays off to do as they pleased. However, many masters forced their slaves to attend church (though they had to sit separately, typically in the back of the room or in an overpacked balcony). Through all of this oppression, a slave culture began to emerge. It was a counterculture, existing in secret opposition to the dominant society.

Legally, slaves were forbidden to marry. This did not stop them. Slaves would often raise families in near secret. Families were frequently torn apart when slaves were sold.

> **[Jim] was saying how the first thing he would do when he got to a free State he would to saving up money and never spend a single cent, and when he got enough he would buy his wife, which was owned on a farm close to where Miss Watson lived; and then they would both work to buy the two children.**

The Importance of Families and Communities

Slaves embraced the concept of the extended family because it allowed them to retain dignity and was a source of support in the face of unending hardship. Tight communities often existed. If a parent were sold to another owner, the extended family would

At top, an oil painting depicting the grandeur of an early eighteenth-century southern plantation. Typically, only a handful of slaves were allowed to enter the main mansion on a plantation. At bottom, a nineteenth-century photograph of a family standing in front of the slave quarters in Savannah, Georgia. Slaves were usually crammed into meager shacks that often lacked floors.

assume responsibility for raising the child left behind. Slaves created word-of-mouth networks for communication. Though most slaves were illiterate, they would find ways to share news.

Slave Counterculture

Nearly everything about the counterculture provided alternatives to existing white myths about blacks. Slaves had their own medicine in the form of herbal remedies. Slaves had their own entertainment in the forms of stories and songs. They held their own religious ceremonies. Most slave owners tolerated these practices if they thought that they would keep the slaves content.

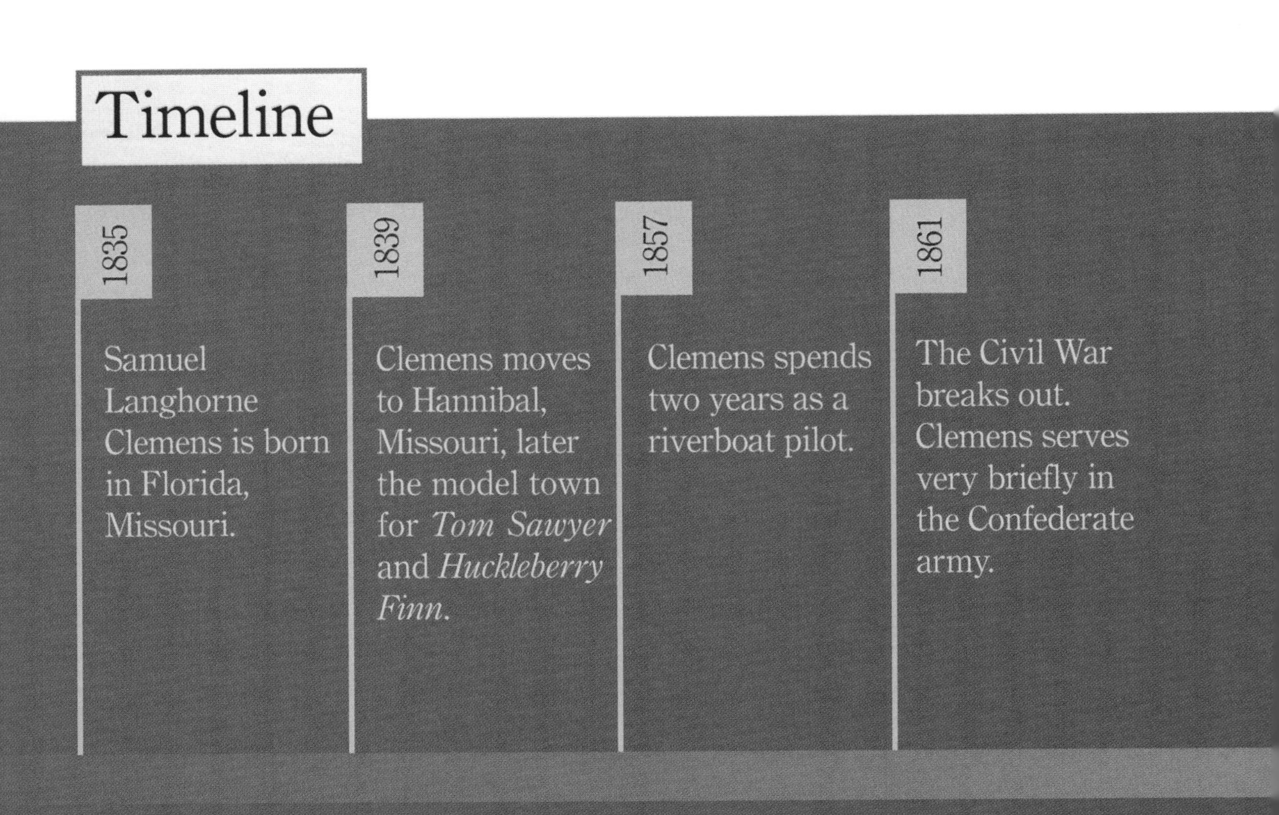

Jim is quite superstitious. Oftentimes, he let "signs" guide him.

> **Some young birds come along, flying a yard or two at a time and lighting. Jim said it was a sign it was going to rain. He said it was a sign when young chickens flew that way, and so he reckoned it was the same way when young birds done it. I was going to catch some of them, but Jim wouldn't let me. He said it was death. He said his father laid mighty sick once, and some of them catched a bird, and his old granny said his father would die, and he did . . .**

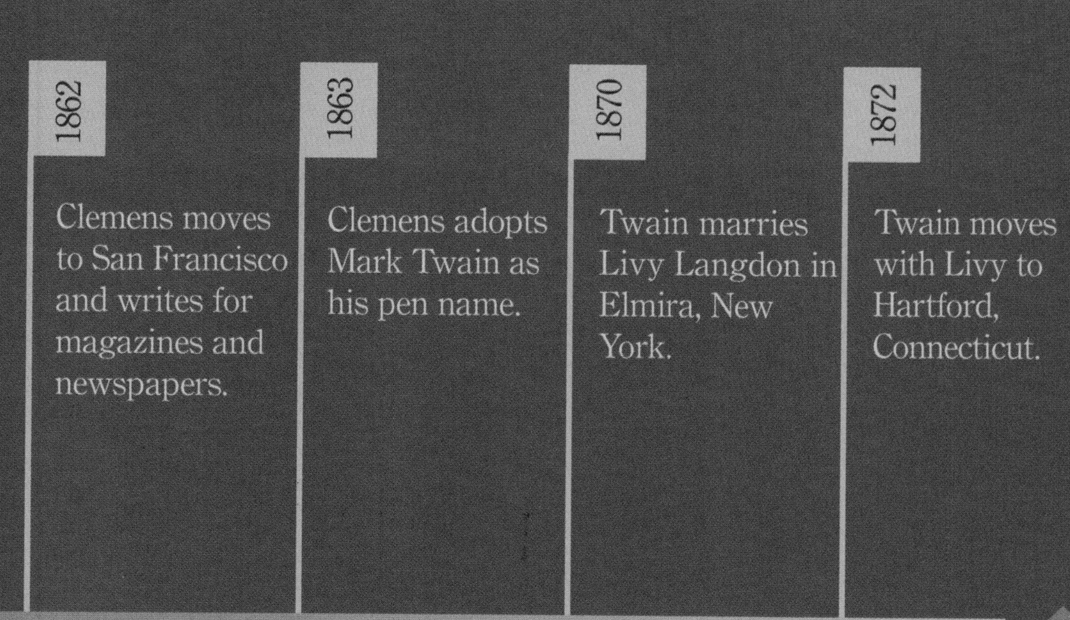

I had heard some of these things before, but not all of them. Jim knowed all kinds of signs. He said he knowed most everything.

Huck is also quite superstitious at times. "One morning I happened to turn over the salt-cellar at breakfast," he says early on in the book. "I reached for some of it as quick as I could, to throw over my left shoulder and keep off the bad luck."

Slave Folklore

One important reason for the development of slave folklore is that it was phrased in allegory. Truths about the issues of life

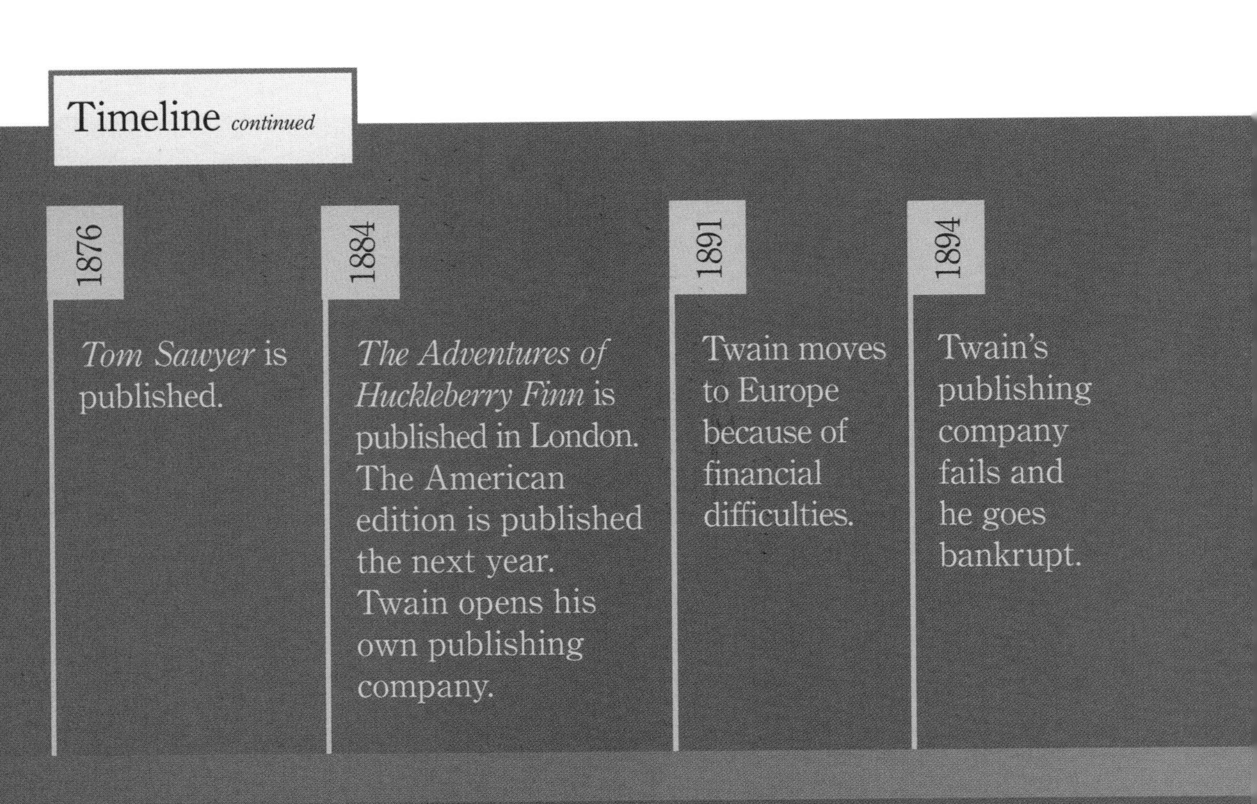

were presented as fictional characters. Everything represented something else. When Jim speaks of one thing, he is really speaking of another. Slaves could not openly express discontent with their stations in life. They had to speak in code. It was a way of protecting themselves against punishment.

For example, in the book's second chapter, Huck and Tom tease Jim by hanging the slave's hat from a tree branch above him as he sleeps.

> **Afterwards, Jim said the witches bewitched him and put him in a trance, and rode him all over the State, and then set him under the trees again and hung his hat**

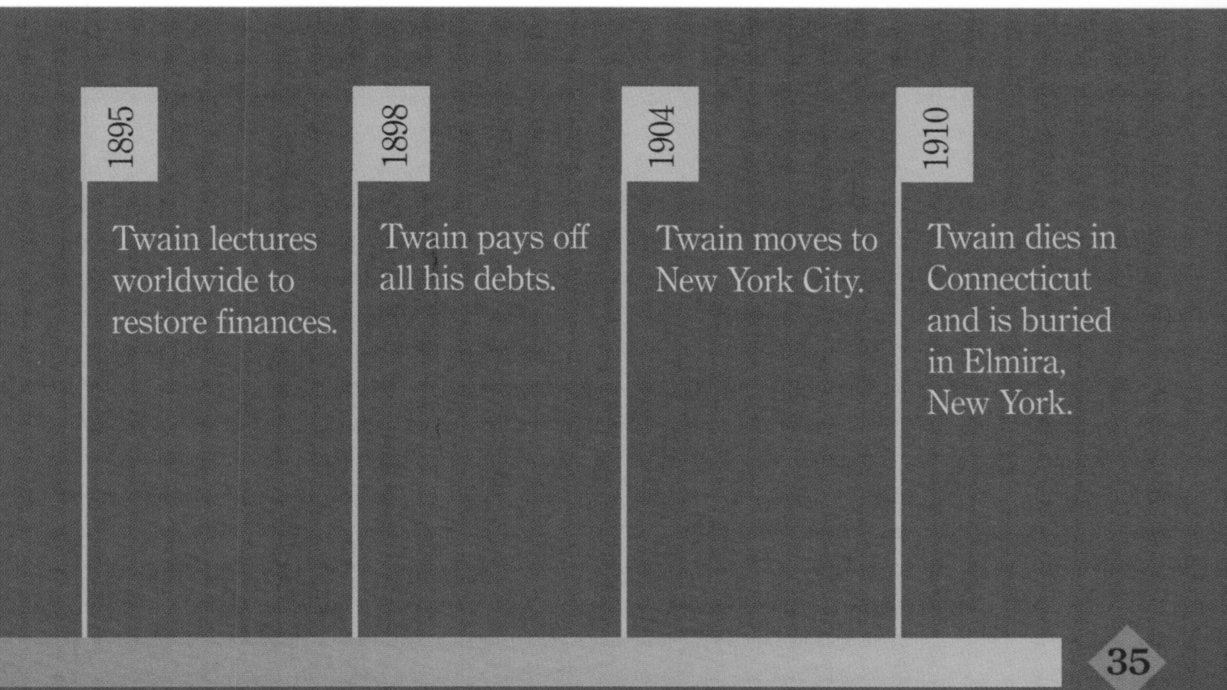

on a limb to show who done it. And next time Jim told it he said they rode him down to New Orleans.

Upon first glance, it appears that Jim has fallen prey to his own superstition. However, it seems more likely that Jim is playing the boys. For slaves, New Orleans, far down the river, was the equivalent of hell. Jim's use of it in his story seems to indicate that he is aware of Tom and Huck's demeaning joke. He uses it as a code to allow him to talk back to his legal superiors without getting in trouble.

Jim's story makes him a celebrity among local slaves. "Jim was most ruined, for a servant," Huck says. "He got so stuck up on account of having seen the devil and been rode by witches." Again, while it appears that Jim is being simply superstitious, he manages to turn the prank to his advantage. The result, for Jim, is that he has to do less work. In the end, it is not Jim who suffers from the prank. It is actually Miss Watson.

These gains were small given the hardship Jim and other slaves had to suffer. Nothing could compare to the grand potential of being a free man, recognized as a human, and owned by no one.

Chapter 4

Abolitionists and the End of Slavery

The abolitionist movement, a drive to end slavery, was slowly building steam in the 1830s. The abolition of slavery was one of the most controversial issues of the day. Even a mention of the word "abolitionist" could stir up trouble. Slave owners were afraid abolitionists would plant the idea of rebellion in slaves' heads.

Slavery in the United States

Slavery was an institution in the United States long before the country won its independence from England. Beginning in 1616, slave traders imported black people from Africa and the Caribbean. They were sold at demeaning auctions and put to work harvesting cotton and tobacco. Exporters shipped the products to England, where they were sold for great profit. The American colonies used this triangle trade to help establish their economies.

In 1808, the United States banned the importation of slaves into the country. Soon, as industrialization took hold, slavery

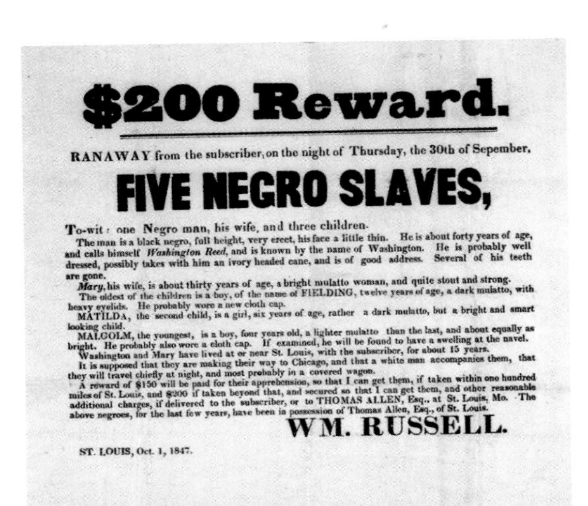
$200 Reward.

RANAWAY from the subscriber, on the night of Thursday, the 30th of Sepember,

FIVE NEGRO SLAVES,

To-wit: one Negro man, his wife, and three children.

The man is a black negro, full height, very erect, his face a little thin. He is about forty years of age, and calls himself *Washington Reed*, and is known by the name of Washington. He is probably well dressed, possibly takes with him an ivory headed cane, and is of good address. Several of his teeth are gone.

Mary, his wife, is about thirty years of age, a bright mulatto woman, and quite stout and strong.

The oldest of the children is a boy, of the name of FIELDING, twelve years of age, a dark mulatto, with heavy eyelids. He probably wore a new cloth cap.

MATILDA, the second child, is a girl, six years of age, rather a dark mulatto, but a bright and smart looking child.

MALCOLM, the youngest, is a boy, four years old, a lighter mulatto than the last, and about equally as bright. He probably also wore a cloth cap. If examined, he will be found to have a swelling at the navel.

Washington and Mary have lived at or near St. Louis, with the subscriber, for about 15 years.

It is supposed that they are making their way to Chicago, and that a white man accompanies them, that they will travel chiefly at night, and most probably in a covered wagon.

A reward of $150 will be paid for their apprehension, so that I can get them, if taken within one hundred miles of St. Louis, and $200 if taken beyond that, and secured so that I can get them, and other reasonable additional charges, if delivered to the subscriber, or to THOMAS ALLEN, Esq., at St. Louis, Mo. The above negroes, for the last few years, have been in possession of Thomas Allen, Esq., of St. Louis.

WM. RUSSELL.

ST. LOUIS, Oct. 1, 1847.

♦♦♦ This reward poster for the return of a family of runaway slaves reads, in part, "It is supposed that they are making their way to Chicago, and that a white man accompanies them, that they will travel chiefly at night, and most probably in a covered wagon."

was abolished in many northern states. By the early 1830s, the abolitionist movement had crept into the public eye. In 1831, William Lloyd Garrison began to circulate *The Liberator*, an abolitionist newspaper, in Boston. It gave a voice to the movement. Within a few years, several other publications had sprung up. Simultaneously, freed slaves in the North began to agitate for abolition. Autobiographies of former slaves testifying to the brutality of slavery also served as evidence.

The Underground Railroad

With discontent brewing, an informal network of safe houses for runaway slaves grew. Houses often had secret rooms where fugitives could be hidden. Slaves and abolitionists spoke in careful code, using signs and signals that allowed them to help transport fellow travelers. The Underground Railroad created a path that enabled slaves to escape from the Deep South to as far north as Canada.

Escaped slaves often traveled the Underground Railroad in wagons like the one pictured here. Driven by white abolitionists, the wagons had a compartment in which slaves hid, covered by bags of grain and other products.

Threats to Freed Slaves

The legal standing of escaped slaves was a shaky one. But so was the standing of those who were freed legally. A series of vicious laws existed to annoy and threaten freed slaves. During his extended rant against the "govment," Huck's father lays into a freed black man.

> **There was a free nigger here, from Ohio, a mulatter, most as white as white man. He had the whitest shirt on you ever see, too, and the shiniest hat; and there ain't**

> **man in that town that's got as fine clothes as what he had; and he had a gold watch and chain, and a silver-headed cane—the awfulest old grey-headed nabob in the State . . . He wouldn't a give me the road if I hadn't shoved him out o' the way. I says to the people, why ain't this nigger put up at auction and sold?—that's what I want to know. And what do you reckon they said? Why, they said he couldn't be sold till he'd been in the State six months, and he hadn't been there that long yet.**

Freed Black Men in Missouri

Freed black men were not allowed to stay in Missouri for more than six months at a time. Government officials were afraid that if they did, they would encourage other slaves to overthrow their masters. There were many other laws as well. For example, in Hannibal, there were many ordinances during Twain's childhood. All free black men needed to have a "permit" from the mayor to prove that they were free. To get the permit, the men needed to show "good moral character and behavior." In addition, they had to pay $5 to the city for the right to use the streets. Likewise, they could not be out after 9 PM without a special pass.

Bounty Hunters

Huck and Jim plan Jim's escape around these laws, though they do not speak of them directly. For example, immediately across the

♦♦♦ **This illustration is also from the original edition of *The Adventures of Huckleberry Finn.* It depicts Duke, a scam artist whom Huck and Jim encounter on their journey.**

river from St. Petersburg is Illinois. While Illinois is technically a free state, it is not wise for Jim to run there. Local officials uphold the Fugitive Slave Act. This act allows slave owners to hire and send bounty hunters to retrieve runaway slaves. Oftentimes, bounty hunters would simply claim that any black man they saw was a runaway slave, kidnap him, and sell him. It is best for Jim to get as far away as possible.

Throughout the book, Huck and Jim must elude such bounty hunters. They do this in a variety of ways—occasionally in ridiculous ways. At one point, two bounty hunters approach the raft. As Jim hides in the cabin, Huck convinces them that his father is sick with smallpox and they go away. Later, when Huck, the King, and the Duke have to leave Jim alone aboard the raft, the Duke concocts a plan.

> **He was uncommon bright, the Duke was, and he soon struck it. He dressed Jim up in a King Lear's outfit—it was a long curtain-calico gown, and a white horse-hair wig and whiskers; and then he took his theatre-paint and painted Jim's face and hands and ears and neck all over a dead dull solid blue, like a man that's been drownded nine days. Blamed if he warn't the horriblest looking outrage I ever see. Then the Duke took and wrote out a sign on a shingle so—Sick Arab—but harmless when not out of his head.**

In the end, it is a legal turn that allows Jim to be freed. After Tom Sawyer's outlandish scheme to free Jim goes awry, Tom stands up for him, and eventually Jim is set free.

> **"Turn him loose! He ain't no slave; he's as free as any cretur that walks this earth!"**
> **"What does that child mean?"**
> **"I mean every word I say, Aunt Sally . . . I've knowed him all his life, and so has [Huck] there. Old Miss Watson died two months ago, and she was ashamed she ever was going to sell him down the river, and said so; and she set him free in her will."**

Close to 198,000 black men served in the Union army and navy during the American Civil War. This photograph shows a company of armed black soldiers at Fort Lincoln in the District of Columbia in 1865.

The abolitionist movement continued in the 1840s and 1850s, gaining supporters in both northern and southern quarters.

The End of Slavery

It was not the abolitionist movement, though, that led to the eruption of the Civil War. An intricate group of causes, mostly centered around the rights of the states to make their own choices, eventually led nearly a dozen states to secede from the Union, thus beginning the bloody war.

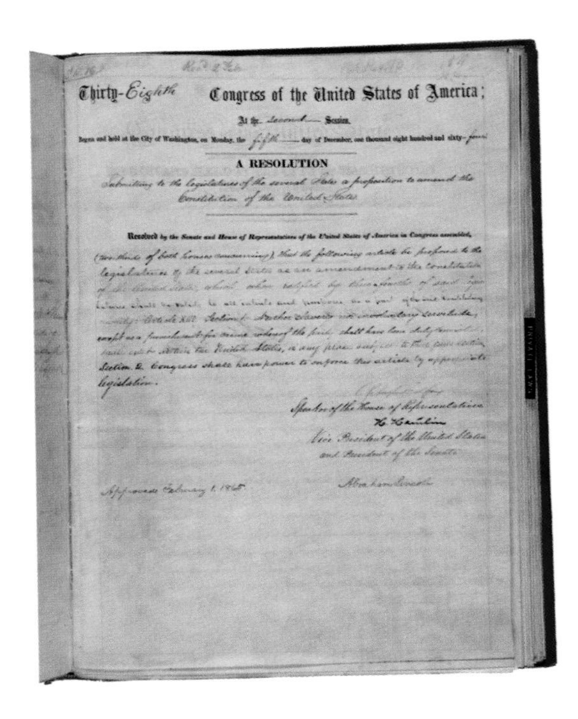
Thirty-Eighth Congress of the United States of America;

At the Second Session.

Begun and held at the City of Washington, on Monday, the fifth day of December, one thousand eight hundred and sixty-four

A RESOLUTION

Submitting to the legislatures of the several States a proposition to amend the Constitution of the United States.

Resolved by the Senate and House of Representatives of the United States of America in Congress assembled,

Section 2. Congress shall have power to enforce this article by appropriate legislation.

Speaker of the House of Representatives

Vice President of the United States and President of the Senate

Approved February 1, 1865

◆◆◆ **The Thirteenth Amendment is one of three so-called Civil War Amendments that were adopted after the Civil War and were intended to expand the civil rights of African Americans.**

The Emancipation Proclamation

By the time the battles ended, President Abraham Lincoln had issued the Emancipation Proclamation, which ended slavery in the South. Originally the famed Emancipation Proclamation was merely a political maneuver on the part of President Lincoln. He wanted to weaken the South by depleting its manpower, as well as boost the reputation of the Union in the eyes of European countries. Neither France nor Britain, who had already abolished slavery, had recognized the Confederacy. The Emancipation Proclamation assured that they never would.

There were some doubts about the Emancipation Proclamation being constitutional. But this issue was soon resolved. In 1865, the Thirteenth Amendment to the Constitution was enacted, abolishing slavery throughout the United States. Though slavery as an institution no longer existed, racism still continued throughout the South and the North.

Chapter 5

Twain Challenges Southern Myths

The Adventures of Huckleberry Finn is not an argument against slavery. The institution had already been abolished for more than ten years by the time Twain began writing the book in 1876. At that time, the South was nearing the end of the period known as Reconstruction. The Civil War had left the South devastated. The land was in ruins. The economic system, driven by slave labor, was obliterated. Hundreds of thousands of former slaves had no money and nowhere to go.

Reconstruction in the South

Reconstruction was a success at first. Thousands of black children attended school for the first time (as did many white children, for that matter). The Fourteenth and Fifteenth Amendments to the Constitution guaranteed blacks the right to vote. Two black members were elected to the United States Senate. But racism was far from gone, in both the South and the North. Though there was no more slavery, it persisted in other forms. The so-called black codes sought to keep former slaves in

During Reconstruction, a number of African Americans were elected to the United States Senate and House of Representatives, as well as state and local offices such as governor and mayor. The men pictured in this 1872 portrait were the first black congressmen in United States history.

conditions similar to slavery, leaving them far below the poverty line. The newly established Ku Klux Klan terrorized blacks across the South.

Though Jim is very much a slave, his hopes and dreams are attached to the promises of Reconstruction.

> **"You know dat one-laigged nigger dat b'longs to old Misto Bradish? Well, he sot up a bank, en say anybody dat put in a dollar would git fo' dollars mo' at de en' er de year. Well, all de niggers went in, but de didn' have much."**

This woodcut depicts members of the Ku Klux Klan deciding on the execution of a black man in North Carolina in 1871. The Ku Klux Klan was first established in 1865 by a group of Confederate war veterans.

Slave "banks" were virtually nonexistent. Twain is referring to the Freedman's Bank, established after the Civil War for ex-slaves, which failed in the early 1870s.

The End of Reconstruction

In 1877, after a widely disputed election, Rutherford B. Hayes became president. As part of a deal that allowed him to win, Hayes agreed to end many Reconstruction policies. Soon, the South set in place a new wave of segregation laws. Reconstruction was effectively ended. It was during this period that Mark Twain did the bulk of the work on *Huckleberry Finn*. Segregation continued to grow, as did Twain's indignation.

The Real State of the Union

Though not about slavery, much of Twain's writing commented on the state of the Union as it stood in the 1870s and 1880s. Particularly offensive to Twain was the romantic vision of the antebellum South that was then sweeping popular culture. Books and plays were filled with happy slaves working under plantation owners who acted like feudal lords. Twain saw that people were creating a happy image of a South that had never existed. The second section of *Huckleberry Finn*, written between 1879 and 1880, takes particular aim at the hypocrisy.

Much of the romanticism involved a set of "noble values" that the authors claimed existed before the Civil War. Questioning whether these values ever existed, Twain framed them in the family feud between the Grangerfords and the Sheperdsons. Huck explains the origins of the feud.

> **Col. Grangerford was a gentleman, you see. He was a gentleman all over; and so was his family. He was well born, as the saying is . . .**
>
> **Every day of his life he put on a clean shirt and a full suit from head to foot made out of linen so white it hurt your eyes to look at it; and on Sundays he wore a blue tail-coat with brass buttons on it. He carried a**

This illustration, entitled *On the Raft,* appeared in the original edition of *Huckleberry Finn.* The artist, Edward Kemble, became one of the leading illustrators of black characters following his work on Twain's novel.

mahogany cane with a silver head to it. There warn't no frivolishness about him, not a bit, and he warn't ever loud . . . When him and the old lady come down in the morning, all the family got up out of their chairs and give them good-day, and didn't set down again till they had set down . . . they bowed and said "Our duty to you, sir, and madam."

Though they act like royalty, the Grangerfords are still relentless in their attempt to kill the Sheperdson family so that they may defend their honor. However, nobody can remember how the feud began. Huck witnesses senseless deaths while he is with them, including that of his new friend, Buck.

Smart and Compassionate Jim

Twain attempted to penetrate the hypocrisy of racism by creating Jim, a smart, compassionate black man. Though some have accused Twain of portraying Jim as a stereotype, the book does not bear this out. Throughout the book, Huck reveals the implicitly racist nature of his upbringing. Though Huck has enough common sense to know better, it is as if Jim must win him over during their journey. Near the end of the novel, Huck reflects on their relationship.

[I] got to thinking over our trip down the river. And I see Jim before me, all the time, in the day, and in the

Biased Laws

Slavery was straightforward. Whites owned and controlled blacks. With the abolition of slavery, racism took on terrible new forms. The most visible, throughout the nineteenth and twentieth centuries, were the Jim Crow laws. The name was derived from the same sort of blackface minstrel shows that Twain satirizes in *Huckleberry Finn*. The laws defrauded blacks out of their constitutional rights. The most widespread of these rules was established by the Supreme Court case *Plessy v. Ferguson* (1896), which declared that businesses had to provide "separate but equal" facilities for blacks and whites, such as school, hotels, dining counters, water fountains, and bathrooms.

Brown v. the Board of Education (1954) overturned *Plessy v. Ferguson*. John F. Kennedy's Civil Rights Act, passed after his death, made it illegal to discriminate against black voters. Thanks to countless civil rights leaders, such as Martin Luther King Jr., great inroads were made throughout the 1960s. Again, the new laws tried their best, though they still didn't eliminate racist practices.

An Act

To promote the comfort of passengers on Railway trains; requiring all Railway companies carrying passengers on their trains, in the State, to provide equal but separate accommodations for the white and colored races, by providing separate coaches or compartments so as to secure separate accommodations, &c.

ORIGINATED

IN THE

House of Representatives.

Clerk of the House of Representatives.

Received in the office of the Secretary of State July 10. 1890

Secretary of State

Received, Baton Rouge,

This is the first page of Louisiana's Separate Car Act, which was at the center of the *Plessy v. Ferguson* Supreme Court case.

night-time, sometimes moonlight, sometimes storms, and we a floating along, talking, and singing, and laughing. But somehow I couldn't seem to strike no places to harden me against him, but only the other kind. I'd see him standing my watch on top of his'n, stead of calling me, so I could go on sleeping; and see him how glad he was when I come back out of the fog; and when I come to him again in the swamp, up there where the feud was; and such-like times; and would always call me honey, and pet me, and do everything he could think of for me, and how good he always was; and at last I struck the time I saved him by telling the men we had small-pox aboard, and he was so grateful, and said I was the best friend Jim ever had in the world, and the only one he's got now.

Jim is Huck's genuine friend. Huck realizes that not only is he a fellow human being, he is also a good human being. It is an argument that Twain hopes the reader will accept. When Tom Sawyer is accidentally shot during his misfiring scheme to "free" Jim, it is Jim who helps the doctor save Tom. The doctor says the following:

"When I got to where I found the boy, I see I couldn't cut the bullet out without some help, and he warn't in no condition for me to leave, I says, I got to have help,

This photograph shows Mark Twain receiving an honorary doctor of letters degree at Oxford University in Oxford, England, on June 26, 1907.

somehow; and the minute I says it, out crawls this nigger from somewheres, and says he'll help, and he done it', too, and done it very well . . . So there I had to stick, plumb till daylight this morning; and I never see a nigger that was a better nuss or faithfuller; and yet he was resking his freedom to do it, and was all tired out, too."

Twain's Popularity

Though some of Twain's antiracist arguments might seem racist in light of the civil rights reforms of the mid-twentieth century, they were quite revolutionary at the time.

Twain's standing was as a popular author. His works were sold by subscription and could be found in homes all across the country. In a country that continues to struggle with issues surrounding race, the book makes its arguments incredibly well in the twenty-first century. What's more, Twain's characters remain wonderfully rendered, hilarious, and human. Though they were born well over a hundred years ago, they continue to dance jauntily off the page.

Glossary

abolition The banishment or ending of a practice such as slavery.

allegory An artwork in which characters and places are symbols for other things, which gives the work a deeper meaning.

antebellum The years before a war. (From Latin, *ante* meaning "before," and *bellum* meaning "war.")

counterculture A group of people who believe in a system of values that are opposite to the dominant culture of a society.

dialect A method of speaking native to a particular area.

emancipation The act of freeing somebody from captivity.

epithet A word or phrase used in place of the name of a person or thing; an abusive or insulting word or phrase.

feud A long-standing disagreement or fight.

hypocrisy Falsely claiming to have high principles.

industrialization The process by which a nation moves from a farming to a manufacturing economy.

parody An artwork that copies another in a deliberately comical way.

phonetic Pronouncing a word exactly the way it is spelled.

plantation A large farm operated by a system of workers and overseers.

satire A method of using humor to expose society's follies.

slavery A system of enforced labor.

temperance Moderation or abstinence from drinking alcohol.

For More Information

The Mark Twain House
351 Farmington Avenue
Hartford, CT 06105
(860) 247-0998, ext. 26
Web site: http://www.marktwainhouse.org

Mark Twain Museum
208 Hill Street
Hannibal, MO 63401-3316
(573) 221-9010
Web site: http://www.marktwainmuseum.org

Mark Twain Papers and Project
University of California at Berkeley
480 Doe Library
Berkeley, CA 94720-6000
(510) 642-6480
Web site: http://bancroft.berkeley.edu/MTP

Web Sites

Due to the changing nature of Internet links, the Rosen Publishing Group, Inc., has developed an online list of Web sites related to the subject of this book. This site is updated regularly. Please use this link to access the list:

http://rosenlinks.com/lal/hucf

For Further Reading

Hamilton, Virginia, and Leo Dillon. *Many Thousands Gone: African Americans from Slavery to Freedom*. New York: Knopf, 2002.

Kaplan, Justin. *Mr. Clemens and Mark Twain: A Biography.* New York: Touchstone, 1966.

Twain, Mark. *The Adventures of Huckleberry Finn*. New York: Penguin, 2003.

Twain, Mark. *The Adventures of Tom Sawyer*. New York: Viking Press, 1987.

Twain, Mark. *Life on the Mississippi*. New York: Bantam, 1983.

Bibliography

Bates, George E., Jr. *Historic Lifestyles in the Upper Mississippi River Valley*. Lanham, MD: University Press of America, 1983.

Greene, Lorenzo J., Gary R. Kremer, and Antonio F. Holland. *Missouri's Black Heritage*. Columbia, MO: University of Missouri Press, 1993.

Kaplan, Justin. *Mr. Clemens and Mark Twain: A Biography.* New York: Touchstone, 1966.

Mailer, Norman. *The Time of Our Time*. New York: Random House, 1998.

Morrison, Toni. *Re-Marking Twain*. New York: Oxford University Press, 1996.

Smith, David L. "Huck, Jim, and American Racial Discourse." *Mark Twain: A Collection of Critical Essays.* Eric J. Sundquist, ed. Englewood Cliffs, NJ: Prentice Hall, 1984.

Twain, Mark. *The Annotated Huckleberry Finn*. Michael Patrick Hearn, ed. New York: W. W. Norton and Company, 1981.

Primary Source Image List

Cover (top): Portrait of Samuel Clemens (Mark Twain), taken sometime between 1900 and 1910. Housed at the Mark Twain House in Hartford, Connecticut.

Cover (bottom left): Photograph of slaves picking cotton in Savannah, Georgia, circa 1860. Housed at the New-York Historical Society.

Cover (bottom right): Cover of the first edition of *The Adventures of Huckleberry Finn* by Mark Twain. Published in 1885. Housed at the Mark Twain House in Hartford, Connecticut.

Page 6: Illustrated page from the first edition of *The Adventures of Huckleberry Finn*, published in 1885.

Page 8: Lithograph of the town of Hannibal, created by Albert Ruger in 1869. Housed at the Library of Congress in Washington, D.C.

Page 9: Portrait of Samuel Clemens, taken around 1850. Housed at the Mark Twain Project at the University of California at Berkeley.

Page 11: A section of a page from the *Territorial Enterprise* of February 3, 1863, bearing an article written by Mark Twain. Housed at the Mark Twain Project at the University of California at Berkeley.

Page 12: The first installment of *Old Times on the Mississippi* by Mark Twain as published in the *Atlantic Monthly* in January 1875. Housed at the Library of Congress.

Page 16: Clemens's family portrait, taken in the early to middle 1880s. Housed at the Mark Twain House in Hartford, Connecticut.

Page 20: *Cutting and Harvesting Sugar Cane on a Plantation in Louisiana*, nineteenth-century engraving. Artist unknown. Part of a private collection.

Page 22: Illustration of Miss Watson by Edward Windsor Kemble, as published in the first edition of *The Adventures of Huckleberry Finn*. Part of the Barrett Collection.

Page 24: Page from the original draft of *The Adventures of Huckleberry Finn*, with edits by Mark Twain. Housed in the Rare Book Room at the Buffalo and Erie County Public Library in Buffalo, New York.

Page 27: *Jim and the Ghost*, illustration by E. W. Kemble, published in the first edition of *The Adventures of Huckleberry Finn* in 1885. Part of the Rare Books & Manuscript Collection of the New York Public Library.

Page 31 (top): *Louisiana Plantation Scene*, oil on canvas by M. L. Pilsbury. Created around 1860. Housed at the Ogden Museum of Southern Art, University of New Orleans in Louisiana.

Page 31 (bottom): Sepia photograph of a family of slaves in front of slave quarters, nineteenth century. Housed at the New-York Historical Society.

Page 38: Poster announcing a reward for the return of runaway slaves, published in St. Louis, Missouri, on October 1, 1847.

Page 41: Illustration of the Duke by E. W. Kemble, published in the original edition of *The Adventures of Huckleberry Finn* in 1885. Part of the Rare Books & Manuscripts Collection at the New York Public Library.

Page 43: Photograph of the Fourth Colored Infantry at Fort Lincoln, District of Columbia, in 1865. Taken by William Morris Smith.

Page 44: The Thirteenth Amendment of the Constitution of the United States. Housed in the National Archives and Records Administration in Washington, D.C.

Page 47: Group portrait of the first African American congressmen, lithograph, published by Currier & Ives in 1872. Housed in the Library of Congress Prints and Photographs Division in Washington, D.C.

Page 50: *On the Raft*, illustration by E. W. Kemble from the original edition of *The Adventures of Huckleberry Finn*. Published in 1885. Part of the Rare Books & Manuscript Collection at the New York Public Library.

Page 53: Cover page of Louisiana's Separate Car Act of 1890.

Page 55: Photograph of Mark Twain receiving an honorary degree at Oxford University, England, on June 26, 1907.

Index

About the Author

Jesse Jarnow is a freelance writer who lives in New York City.

Photo Credits

Cover (top), p. 47 Library of Congress Prints and Photographs Division; cover (bottom left), p. 31 (bottom) New-York Historical Society, New York, USA/Bridgeman Art Library; cover (bottom right), pp. 6, 27, 41, 50 courtesy of the Rare Books & Manuscripts Collection, New York Public Library Astor, Lenox, and Tilden Foundations; p. 8 Library of Congress, Geography and Map Division; pp. 9, 11 courtesy, The Mark Twain Project, The Bancroft Library; p. 12 (left) Library of Congress, The Nineteenth Century in Print, Periodicals Collection; p. 12 (right) Private Collection/ Bridgeman Art Library; p. 16 The Mark Twain House, Hartford, Connecticut; p. 18 © Corbis; p. 20 Private Collection/Bridgeman Art Library; p. 22 an illustration by E. W. Kemble from the original 1885 edition of *The Adventures of Huckleberry Finn*; p. 24 Reproduction by permission of The Buffalo & Erie County Library, Buffalo, New York; p. 31 (top) Gift of the Roger Houston Ogden Collection, The Ogden Museum of Southern Art, University of New Orleans; p. 38 Library of Congress Rare Book and Special Collections Division; p. 39 courtesy of the Levi Coffin House Association and Waynet.org; pp. 43, 55 © Bettmann/Corbis; p. 44 General Records of the United States Government, Record Group 11, National Archives and Records Administration; p. 48 © North Wind Picture Archives; p. 53 © State of Louisiana, Secretary of State Division of Archives, Records, and History.

Designer: Les Kanturek; Editor: Jill Jarnow;
Photo Researcher: Rebecca Anguin-Cohen